Lotions,

Ointments

And

Salves

These are the recipes of

_____

Lotion Recipes

Recipe #1

Recipe #2

Recipe #3

Recipe #4

Recipe #5

Recipe #6

Recipe #7

Recipe #8

Recipe #9

Recipe #10

Recipe #1

Ingredients

Instructions

Recipe #2

Ingredients

Instructions

Recipe #3

Ingredients

Instructions

Recipe #4

Ingredients

Recipe #5

Ingredients

Instructions

Recipe #6

Ingredients

Instructions

Recipe #7

Ingredients

Recipe #8

Ingredients

Instructions

Recipe #9

Ingredients

Recipe #10

Ingredients

Ointment Recipes

Recipe #1

Recipe #2

Recipe #3

Recipe #4

Recipe #5

Recipe #6

Recipe #7

Recipe #8

Recipe #9

Recipe #10

Recipe #1

Ingredients

Instructions

Recipe #2

Ingredients

Recipe #3

Ingredients

Instructions

Recipe #4

Ingredients

Recipe #5

Ingredients

Instructions

Recipe #6

_____

Ingredients

_____

_____

_____

_____

_____

_____

_____

_____

_____

Instructions

Recipe #7

Ingredients

Instructions

Recipe #8

Ingredients

Instructions

Recipe #9

Ingredients

Instructions

Recipe #10

Ingredients

Instructions

Salve Recipes

Recipe #1

Recipe #2

Recipe #3

Recipe #4

Recipe #5

Recipe #6

Recipe #7

Recipe #8

Recipe #9

Recipe #10

Recipe #1

Ingredients

Recipe #2

Ingredients

Instructions

Recipe #3

Ingredients

Recipe #4

Ingredients

Recipe #5

Ingredients

Recipe #6

Ingredients

Instructions

Recipe #7

Ingredients

Instructions

Recipe #8

Ingredients

Instructions

Recipe #9

Ingredients

Recipe #10

Ingredients

Instructions

Notes

Made in United States
North Haven, CT
24 January 2025

64916886R00039